10-2016 Show Me 1600

HAIL!
ANCIENT
CHINESE

Paul C. Challen

Crabtree Publishing Company
www.crabtreebooks.com

Crabtree Publishing Company

www.crabtreebooks.com

Author: Paul Challen
Editor: Lynn Peppas
Project coordinator: Kathy Middleton
Production coordinator: Ken Wright
Prepress technician: Ken Wright
Managing editor: Miranda Smith
Designer: Lorna Phillips
Picture researcher: Clare Newman
Design manager: David Poole
Editorial director: Lindsey Lowe
Children's publisher: Anne O'Daly
Consultant: Dr Paul G. Bahn

This book was produced for Crabtree Publishing Company by Brown Reference Group.

Photographs:
Alamy: David Sanger: p. 6 (center right)
Art Archive: The British Library: p. 4 (bottom right),
    19 (center left)
Bridgeman Art Library: p. 11 (center left), 13 (top left);
    Angus McBride: p. 28 (center left)
Corbis: Christopher Boisvieux: p. 27 (bottom right);
    Catherine Karnow: p. 7 (bottom left); DK Images:
    p. 15 (bottom left)
iStockPhoto: Robert Churchill: p. 7 (bottom right);
    Elizabeth Shoemaker: p. 27 (top right)
Mary Evans Picture Library: p. 15 (top left), 25 (top)
Photolibrary: Japanese Travel Bureau: p. 6 (bottom left);
    Superstock: p. 5 (bottom center), 12 (center)
Science & Society Picture Library: Science Museum:
    p. 24 (bottom left)
Topham: The Granger Collection: p. 16 (bottom right),
    18 (center); Ullstein Bild: p. 13 (bottom right)
Other images by Shutterstock

Library and Archives Canada Cataloguing in Publication

Challen, Paul, 1967-
    Hail! Ancient Chinese / Paul Challen.

(Hail! History)
Includes index.
ISBN 978-0-7787-6621-6 (bound).--ISBN 978-0-7787-6628-5 (pbk.)

    1. China--Civilization--To 221 B.C.--Juvenile literature.
2. China--Civilization--221 B.C.-960 A.D.--Juvenile literature.
I. Title. II. Title: Ancient Chinese. III. Series: Hail! History

DS747.42.C43 2010   j931   C2010-901286-0

Library of Congress Cataloging-in-Publication Data

Challen, Paul C. (Paul Clarence), 1967-
    Hail! Ancient Chinese / Paul Challen.
        p. cm. -- (Hail! History)
    Includes index.
    ISBN 978-0-7787-6621-6 (reinforced lib. bdg. : alk. paper) --
ISBN 978-0-7787-6628-5 (pbk. : alk. paper)
    1. China--Civilization--To 221 B.C.--Juvenile literature. 2. China--
Civilization--221 B.C.-960 A.D.--Juvenile literature. I. Title. II. Title:
Ancient Chinese. III. Series.

    DS741.65.C424 2010
    931--dc22

                                        2010006655

Crabtree Publishing Company

www.crabtreebooks.com   1-800-387-7650

Printed in China/072010/AP20100226

Copyright © **2011 CRABTREE PUBLISHING COMPANY.**
All rights reserved. No part of this publication may be reproduced,
stored in a retrieval system or be transmitted in any form or by
any means, electronic, mechanical, photocopying, recording,
or otherwise, without the prior written permission of
Crabtree Publishing Company. In Canada: We acknowledge the
financial support of theGovernment of Canada through the Book
Publishing Industry Development Program (BPIDP) for our
publishing activities.

Published in Canada
Crabtree Publishing
616 Welland Ave.
St. Catharines, Ontario
L2M 5V6

Published in the United States
Crabtree Publishing
PMB 59051
350 Fifth Avenue, 59th Floor
New York, New York 10118

CONTENTS

YOUR GUIDE TO
ANCIENT CHINA

Welcome to the true facts about one of the oldest civilizations in the world. Beginning with the Xia Dynasty in 2070 BCE, this inventive culture has been ruled by strong emperors and has given the world the gifts of paper, gunpowder, and silk. *HAIL!* reviews China's finest achievements so that you, the reader, can decide for yourself just what makes the country great.

THE SECRET OF CHINA'S SUCCESS

The history of China is as varied and exciting as its geography. We can trace our origins back to a group of small but charismatic tribes. They have grown in population, expanded their territories, and joined together to become the unified China that we know today.

A LAND OF CONTRASTS

From wild mountains and lonely plateaus, barren deserts and high steppes, to fertile lowlands and wind-swept grasslands, China is a land of plenty. Two magnificent rivers, the Yellow and the Yangtze meander across the plains. For centuries, kings and emperors have established their cities on their banks. China defends its borders and manages to keep out the Western world.

IMPERIAL RULE

In 221 BCE, China was united under the rule of the first and greatest emperor of all, Qin Shi Huangdi. This was the beginning of more than 1,500 years of imperial rule that gave China stability and status in the world.

HAIL! QUIZ WHAT MAKES CHINA FAMOUS?

Enter our readers' poll and select your favorite from these five key achievements.

1. CALENDAR SYSTEM

We were the first people to organize time! During the Shang dynasty, our people developed a lunar calendar system based on a period of 60 days. About 500 BCE, a calendar using a solar year of 365 days was invented, which we have followed ever since.

2. INVENTIONS

No one anywhere surpasses our inventors and alchemists. Their technological achievements include gunpowder, chopsticks, umbrellas, kites, ceramics, and the compass.

3. THE GREAT WALL

One of the reasons that China is so great is that its leaders have foresight and know how to look after their citizens. Several emperors have built, rebuilt, and extended the magnificent Great Wall that stretches south for 5,468 miles (8,800 km) from the northern borders of our magnificent empire.

4. CALLIGRAPHY

Calligraphy, our visual method of writing, is one of the most beautiful and artistic ways of communicating in the world today. Legend says that a man called Cangjie (c.2650 BCE) invented this unique method of expression. Legend has it that when he invented the characters, the deities and the ghosts cried.

5. PHILOSOPHY

We have had some very wise men among us. Around 600 BCE, Lao Tzu founded Taoism, a belief system built on harmony with nature and the forces of yin and yang (see p.16). Confucius (551 BCE) taught us that everyone should develop responsibility and follow a moral code.

Submit Your Answer

SEE INSIDE:

Qin Shi Huangdi pp. 8, 10, 14

Silk supply pp. 12

Inventions pp. 24–25

REGULAR CONTRIBUTORS:
Scholar Li Hua, Oracle Ji Hiu, Confucius, Soldier Jin Wu

MEET THE NEIGHBORS

The Chinese civilization grew and flourished in various city-states along the length of the Yellow River. It was the product of many different tribes—there are 56 official ethnic groups in modern-day China. On these pages, *HAIL!* will introduce you to just a few of these peoples, as well as to some of the invaders who also settled in the country.

Hans Down

The Han people were nomads who chose to settle in the south of China and farm the land. In 206 BCE, a Han government worker named Liu Bang founded the powerful Han dynasty, becoming its first emperor. This began a golden age of peace and prosperity that lasted four centuries! Liu Bang set up tax collection, enforced laws, and made sure the canals and roads were kept in good repair.

The Hans are still the largest ethnic group in China.

NOT SO MINOR

The Zhuang people (above) live in southern China. They have had a hard time of it! During the Song era (960—1280 CE), the Han and the Vietnamese invaded their territory. Although the Zhuang resisted, they were defeated and lost their independence. However, they are beginning to integrate with the peoples who have conquered them. They have also kept their identity with customs, such as the Ox Soul Festival, which celebrates the birthday of the King of Oxen.

RIVER TWINS

There would be no China without the Yellow and Yangtze rivers. They provide the water that farmers need to grow crops. As they flow and sometimes spill over their banks, they deposit silt that becomes rich soil. But the rivers are not always so friendly. They often overflow and kill hundreds of thousands of people. In fact, people call the Yellow River "China's Sorrow" because of the love/hate relationship the people have with it.

To Dai For

The Dai people (below) came from southeast China. The first mention of them in Chinese records was during the reign of Wu Di of the Han Dynasty in 109 BCE. They paid tribute to the Han court in the form of gold seals. They even used gold and silver to plate their teeth! The Dai are an agricultural people who developed a sophisticated method of irrigation for growing rice. They also used oxen and elephants to till their land.

WATCH OUT FOR THE MONGOLS!

Over the centuries, China has been invaded many times. The Huns, the Mongols (right), and the Manchurians have all breached the Great Wall. But all three groups admired what they found and settled down to stay. Some have been more influential than others. Under the leadership of Genghis Khan (c.1162–1227), the fearsome Mongols stormed China from the north. By 1260, Genghis Khan's grandson, Kublai Khan, had become Emperor of China as the head of the Yuan Dynasty. He also opened up the country to trade with the rest of the world.

ON THE COUCH
WITH QIN SHI HUANGDI

Qin Shi Huangdi unified China after conquering all other states. He declared himself the first emperor and founded the Qin Dynasty (221–210 BCE). The word "China" comes from the word "Qin" which is pronounced "Chin." He was quick to kill or banish people—particularly scholars—who disagreed with him, and burned the books that remained from past regimes.

Boss of the month!

HAIL! **sat down with Qin Shi Huangdi for an up-close and personal conversation about what it is really like to be Emperor of China.**

 So, how's the wife?

 That's wives, plural. As you obviously don't know, I have many. It's a tradition among Chinese emperors. But thanks for asking; they're fine.

 Right. We wanted to ask you...

 About my "style" as a ruler, right? Basically, it's simple. I'm the emperor. People do what I say. If they don't, I...deal with them!

 Deal with them? What do you mean?

 Let's just say that if they don't agree with me, they're not around much longer to give any trouble.

 Um, right. On a more pleasant topic, can you tell us about work you've done to help the Chinese people?

 Sure. As you know, I've started building a huge wall in the north of the country to keep out invaders. And along with one of my top advisers, a fellow named Li Si, I've developed a bunch of new laws and tax rules that will make sure China stays strong for a long time. Of course, if people don't like the laws and taxes they have to pay...

 Let's finish by saying that we've heard about the project you've given your scholars—the research into the secret of "eternal life."

 We emperors are chosen by the gods. But maybe there is a secret to living forever. So I'm asking my scholars to look into it. And if they don't find it, well...that's it for them!

"I want to find the secret of living forever."

THE LIFE OF A...
SCHOLAR: LI HUA

Hail! **wanted to know how one of the emperor's scholars, "Li Hua" (his name has been changed for obvious reasons), spent his day studying and reflecting on the search for eternal life.**

The High Life

Scholars, or "men of arts," are among the highest ranking people in Chinese society. They have access to the palace, great food, amazing parties. It is a good job—as long as it lasts!

狗
DOG

LEARNING THE TRADE

"Li Hua," like all scholars, is trained in musical instruments, board games, calligraphy, and painting. By combining these talents every day, the scholar becomes a master of creativity and expression and develops extraordinary thinking power. The emperor has directed "Li Hua" to apply his thinking power to the idea of eternal life.

Chime bells

Chinese chess

Traditional painting

Calligraphy

"Li Hua," or any scholar, is nothing without his tools. Chinese calligraphy is a practical technique for writing Chinese characters, like the character for "dog" above, next to that adorable pooch! However, calligraphy is much more than this. It is an expression of the scholar's poetic nature as well as a communication between learned people. Only three basic forms—the square, triangle, and circle—are used to create a character. A set number of brushstrokes are used, but they can have individual style. All of this helps "Li Hua" concentrate his mind and work on the emperor's task—before it is too late.

Our most beloved Emperor Qin Shi Huangdi has been building his giant mausoleum since he was 13 years old. In addition to the chariots, horses, and animals that will accompany him on his journey to the afterlife, he needs an army of more than 8,000 soldiers made of terracotta clay.

HELP WANTED!

Now is your chance to make history! Be a model for one of the clay soldiers being created for the emperor's mausoleum—a tomb that is taking 700,000 workers to build! The emperor wants every soldier to look different, from the way he ties his hair to the expression on his face.

WE'RE LOOKING FOR LOYAL SUBJECTS, WHO ARE FROM 72 INCHES (183 CM) TO 77 INCHES (195 CM) TALL, TO POSE AS:

- ✔ **Generals**
- ✔ **Warriors**
- ✔ **Charioteers**
- ✔ **Officials**
- ✔ **Musicians**
- ✔ **Acrobats**
- ✔ **Strongmen**

DON'T MISS IT!

NO EXPERIENCE NEEDED!

WANTED!

Some loyal folks who will not mind being buried alive in the underground mausoleum— What a way to show your loyalty to the emperor! Officials, retainers (servants), and councillors of all ranks and ages needed!

Hundreds of horses are needed to model as well. Bring your horse along to join the clay army!

APPLY NOW !

Did you know?

The terracotta army was actually discovered by farmers in 1974, in Shaanxi Province. Archaeologists found an estimated 8,000 soldiers, plus hundreds of chariots and horses inside three vaults that were dug up.

ON THE CATWALK
What They're Wearing This Year

In ancient China, everyone can tell what position people hold in society based on what they are wearing. The rich folks wear amazing, colorful tunics made from pure silk. The poor folks need practical clothes made out of tough hemp. Here is a guide to who is wearing what this season.

A sure sign that you are a rich person is that your robes and slippers are made from finest silk.

Silky Smooth

A Chinese legend tells how, in 2460 BCE, 14-year-old Empress Xi Ling Shi took a cocoon from a mulberry tree and found that she could unwind a silk thread. For several centuries, only royalty were allowed to wear silk. Anyone else caught wearing silk would be punished with death.

The silk supply

Silkworms spend three or four days spinning a cocoon round themselves until they look like fluffy white balls (right). The cocoons are steamed or baked to kill the worms, then dipped in hot water to loosen the threads. The threads are unwound onto a spool. Each cocoon produces up to 1,000 yards (914 m) of thread!

What is hemp?

Hemp is a soft, durable fiber that comes from a plant. Peasants use it to make their clothing and rope.

The Peasant Look

It is hard working in the fields all day! You need comfort for all that hoeing and harvesting. And it is important to stay cool in the summer and warm in winter. That is why the well-dressed rural guy or gal sports a loose-fitting, shirt-like garment (left) made of wool or hemp. You can also cover your head against the elements. Complete the look with shoes made of straw.

WHAT'S AFOOT?

One of the strangest fashions in ancient China is the practice of binding the feet of young girls with long strips of cloth. The idea is that the most attractive feet for women are very small ones. Rich people hoping to make good marriages for their daughters use this method to stop the feet of young girls from growing. Of course, this hurts... a lot! Only farming families, who need their daughters to stay active for farm work, do not follow this fashion.

WHAT THE RICH FOLKS WEAR

If you are a nobleman or woman, or a high-ranking official, you have your status in society to maintain. And what is the good of your having lots of extra cash to spend if you cannot show off your wealth? Silk robes and gold, silver, or jade jewelry on your wrists or around your neck will give you that extra fashionable look.

Jade

Gold nuggets

DEAR DIARY

Construction on Qin Shi Huangdi's Great Wall of China was started in 221 BCE. The emperor built the wall because he knew China needed to defend itself against invasion from the north by the dreaded Mongols.

A SOLDIER'S LIFE

Jin Wu is a guard on the Great Wall. He is 19 years old and has been guarding the wall for two years. "It is tough work," says Jin, "but a great honor to protect the country against invaders." As the son of poor peasants from the south, Jin considers guarding the wall "the best job a guy like me could hope for." He especially likes the food served in the guards' quarters and working with his friends.

BUILDING THE WALL

The Chinese have heard tell of wonders in the West such as the Great Pyramid in Egypt and the Colosseum in Rome. But nothing is as amazing as our Great Wall. During Emperor Qin Shi Huangdi's reign, we have fought off nomadic tribes such as the Xiongnu in the north and northwest. However, they are still trying to invade, so the emperor has ordered this impressive defensive wall to be built. It will stretch more than 2,250 miles (3,469 km) across northern China.

The wall was first built with wood by peasant laborers, but was later rebuilt using stone and bricks.

Thursday

December 205 BCE

4 am Wake-up call
4:30 am Exercises to get ready for the day
5 am Breakfast—millet and milk porridge
5:30 to 11:30 am Guarding the wall
11:30 am to noon Lunch break—wheat noodles and bean curd
Noon to 7 pm Not a sign of those invaders that everyone keeps warning us about, and it's freezing cold on the wall!

7 pm Turn over post to night-shift guard
7:30 pm Dinner of rice and chicken
8 pm: Music lesson—I am learning to play the flute
9 pm: And so to bed!

Did you know?

A series of walls were built between the 5th century BCE and the 16th century CE. The majority of the wall that exists in 2010 CE was built during the Ming Dynasty (1368–1644).

What a wall!

In Chinese, the Great Wall is called "Chángchéng," which means "long fortress." In most parts, it has a wide area for foot traffic across the top. Signal towers were built on hill tops so that the soldiers could signal to army units in barracks along the wall whenever there was trouble.

ON THE OTHER SIDE?

Qin Shi Huangdi's Great Wall is designed to keep out invaders. The most notorious of these are the Mongols. The Mongols come from the area just to the north of China and are well-known for their fighting skills. They have a long history of conflict with the Chinese on the northern border and with many other peoples who live in that area. The Mongols are especially feared for their ability to shoot with bows and arrows even while riding fast on horseback!

HOROSCOPES

Astrology plays a significant role in Chinese culture. The horoscope, with its 12 different animals representing the 12-year cycle of the Chinese lunar calendar, was built on a foundation of astronomy and ancient Chinese philosophy.

TAO IS IT!

It is 440 BCE, and Taoism has just become a national religion in China! A scholar named Lao Tzu (born c.600 BCE) created this belief system to end a series of wars in China. Taoism emphasizes harmony with nature. It also teaches that the forces of yin and yang—the symbols for which are shown here—are the opposing forces in the Universe.

Roll the bones

One way to predict the future is by using oracle bones. These were first used in China in 1400 BCE, when priests, or oracles, in the Shang Dynasty carved questions to the gods on turtle shells and sheep bones (right). They are now increasingly popular with the general public.

It is a zoo out there!

The Chinese have a system for keeping track of the years. It is called the zodiac. Legend has it that the Buddha once called all the animals of China together, but only 12 of them showed up. To reward them, he named a year after each one. Since each of the animals has its own character traits, people born in that year are supposed to also have the characteristics of that animal.

WHATEVER HAPPENED TO UNCLE JIN?

The ancient Chinese believe that they can pray to the spirits of their dead ancestors, and these ancestors will guide and help them. In most homes, people have set up an altar where offerings such as fruit and specially prepared food and drink can be made to these relatives. Letters and greetings expressing veneration for the ancestor are also put on the altars.

HE KNOWS WHAT IS GOING TO HAPPEN

Do you?

HAIL! spoke to Chinese oracle Ji Hui to find out how he uses oracle bones to predict the future.

So, you've got amazing oracle bones. Can you give us a demonstration of how they work?

Certainly! I start with two statements: "Next year's rice crop will be good," and "Next year's rice crop will be bad."

Right. What then?

Each of my oracle bones is divided into two halves—a positive and a negative. There is a hole in each half, and when I heat up the bones with my special burning stick, the holes cause the bones to crack.

OK, then what?

Then I read the cracks to see what they tell me about next year's crop.

And what are they telling you?

Ah, well, that's kind of a trade secret that only we oracles know.

You can burn special "spirit" money for your ancestors to use!

Buddha is boss

Based on the teachings of the Buddha, or the "Enlightened One," the religion Buddhism is spreading across China. Buddhism teaches that people can be happy only when they stop wanting material possessions, which lead to suffering.

WELCOME TO
CHANG'AN

Chang'an (modern name Xi'an) was an important city in ancient China. Emperor Liu Bang established it as a capital city "at the center of the world" in 202 BCE. It was also the eastern end of the Silk Road, a trade route between China and the Mediterranean.

WHAT'S TO SEE?

Chang'an is famous for its magnificent buildings, but there are none more amazing than the Small Wild Goose Pagoda. Its base is made from packed earth in the shape of a hemisphere to spread the pressure when there is an earthquake. Despite damage in the city, the pagoda remains standing!

Quick Facts

Running short on time? Just passing through? Here are some fast facts on this famous city:

✔ Capital city during ten Chinese dynasties, including the Han (206–220 BCE) and the Tang (618–907 CE)

✔ Political and military center of China during this time

✔ More than one million inhabitants at its peak

✔ The name Chang'an means "perpetual peace" in classical Chinese

✔ The city is protected by a 16-mile-(26 km) long wall

Quick Facts

TOP SPOT

HOT REVIEW—WHERE TO EAT

Make the most of your contacts while in town. Stop off at Liu Bang's sumptuous Weiyang Palace for a feast. You can dine on pork, lamb, duck, pigeon, snake, dog, bear paws, and rice. If you are there on the right day, there will also be sea food from the coast!

Rating: ★★★★☆

CITY FOUNDER

Known as Emperor Goazu of Han, Liu Bang is an unusual leader because he is one of the few emperors to come from peasant stock. He is known for his bravery, and it is said he once killed a cobra that had poisonous breath and was larger than a fully grown tree! Liu Bang has made Chang'an his showpiece city.

Tourist Heaven

You may have had a difficult journey to Chang'an with all the bandits on the road, but during your stay here, you can feel very safe. The impressive wall that surrounds the city is guarded night and day against invaders. In some places it is more than 17 yards (15.5 m) thick at the base!

ASK CONFUCIUS

The scholar Confucius lived from 551 to 479 BCE. Born in northeastern China, he left his homeland when he was 50 and for 12 years wandered from state to state. He tried to persuade local rulers to follow his teachings, but was unsuccessful. So he returned home and instead trained disciples in his philosophy.

Dear Master:
I am having some confusion at home. My father is always telling me what to do, and I am tired of it. What should I do?

A not-so-loyal son in Louyang

Dear Not-So-Loyal:
You must always obey your father! This family loyalty is the basis for life in our country. It is the same with husbands and wives, and older and younger siblings—all must be loyal to one another. If people stop following these rules of loyalty, China will fall apart!

Dear Master:
I have been hearing stories lately of the emperor becoming too powerful. Is there anything we can do about this?

Concerned
in Zhongdu

Dear Master:
I hate school!
Must I continue
my studies?

Struggling
in Hangzhou

Dear Concerned:
Think of the emperor as the father of a large family. We must always remember that our "father" has our best interests in mind. The care of a just emperor, combined with the loyalty we owe him, is the only path to a peaceful society.

Dear Struggling:
Of course you must! Education is key, not only to your development, but to China as a whole. Good government and the sound administration of our country can only be achieved through education! Stick to it, and help China grow even more strong and powerful.

Dear Master,
I am trying to set one of the
ballads from your collection,
Shi Jing — The Book of Songs,
to music. The ballad is "White
Moonrise," which begins:
    "The white rising moon
    is your bright beauty
    binding me in spells
    till my heart's devoured..."
        I am having an argument
    with another musician about
    whether this should be in
    the style of a folk song
        or a court song.
        Can you help?

            In hope
            Anonymous

Dear Anonymous,
You have chosen well, my son. As you know, I consider that poetry serves a moral purpose. It stimulates the reader and at the same time helps him to serve his family and his king. With this in mind, you should recognize that this is a love song to beauty and expresses the poet's deepest feelings. I think that this poem has been taken from folk song roots. It has been reworked into stanzas now and is very suitable for setting to music as a court song.

China mourns the Master

" **Our greatest glory is not in never falling, but in getting up every time we do.** "

The Master died peacefully at the venerable age of 72. He had dedicated his life to teaching a series of rules that he believed would help people live a good life. Since his death, his sayings have been traveling like wildfire—right to the other side of the world! Quiet, peaceful Confucian temples surrounded by gardens have been springing up all over the place. This one, Wen Miao Temple in Shanghai, is dedicated to the worship of Confucius and the study of his texts.

HOW DOES YOUR
GARDEN GROW?

The Chinese have grown rice for 7,000 years. They cook and eat it, and they make rice wine to supplement their favorite drink—tea. They grow their rice in paddy fields, often on terraces on hillsides.

HOW TO BUILD A RICE TERRACE

1. Find a hill.

2. Use shovels, hoes, rakes, and plows pulled by animals such as water buffaloes to cut "steps" into the hillside. Your hill should now look like a big staircase.

3. Keep these flat steps well weeded and plant rice on them.

4. Water the terraces well.

ON THE TERRACE

From our economics correspondent:
The ancient Chinese farmers have come up with a superb idea for making a profit. They are making maximum use of land by growing rice on hillsides. But the hills are sloped, you say! Well, they are building terraces, which stop erosion. The terraces are nice and flat, so it is easy for people and animals to work on them.

How to Grow Rice

You start by planting the rice seeds in the flooded field. When the plants are about 1 foot (30 cm) tall, move them to the main field, which should be well-plowed and free of weeds. When it is ready to pick, separate the rice kernels from the outside of the seed.

RICE IS NICE!

People need rice so that they can grow, stay healthy, and raise families. Cooked with small pieces of meat and plenty of vegetables from the garden, rice gives the ancient Chinese people all the nutrition and vitamins that they need.

WEATHER WARNING!

Rice grows best in very wet conditions. It may seem strange, but Chinese farmers find it best to flood their paddy fields with water when growing rice.

Grand Opening *618* CE

This superb waterway has just opened, with much fanfare! The Grand Canal runs from Beijing to Hangzhou and, at more than 1,100 miles (1,770 km) in length, it is the largest human-made waterway in the world. Until now, the people in the north of China could not grow rice to eat because it is too dry and cold. They had to make do with wild millet and sorghum! Now rice is sent to the north along the Grand Canal.

The GADGET SHOW

The ancient Chinese invented many of the things that we use today, including the wheelbarrow, paper money, and porcelain china. However, there were four Chinese inventions that had particular impact, not only on China, but on the rest of the world: the compass, gunpowder, paper, and printing.

Masters of Invention

Many people believe that the Confucian philosophy of education has a lot to do with the Chinese genius for inventing. Confucianism states that education is the best way to prepare people to work to serve their country. Invention is a result of education!

Medical treatments

In this country we have the best medical services in the known world! The goal is to keep people healthy—not to focus on curing them when they get sick. Doctors use herbs and treatments, such as acupuncture, to keep the yin and yang of their patients in balance. Acupuncture is the latest and most exciting treatment. Tiny needles are placed in parts of the body, exactly where the energy is flowing.

EARTHQUAKE PREDICTOR

One the most exciting exhibits at this year's show, in 132 CE, is the seismograph. Chang Heng, a brilliant scientist and mathematician, has invented this extraordinary device to predict earthquakes. The eight dragons round the rim hold balls in their mouths. When a dragon drop its ball into the mouth of one of the eight toads below, an earthquake is coming!

The earthquake direction is indicated by the position of the toad that swallows the ball.

FOR SALE
Get your fine wheelbarrows here! Recommended for use in the battlefield by the inventor General Chuko Liang.

WHILE STOCKS LAST!

THE WRITTEN WORD

To record things, you need something to write on. In 105 CE, we came up with the perfect invention! If you mix bamboo with wood, rags, and other things in just the right quantities, you can make "paper" that you can write on. Chinese monks have also developed a way of coating pieces of marble with ink and pressing them onto wet paper, a process that they are calling "printing."

The Right Direction

Since earliest times, Chinese fortune-tellers have used naturally magnetized lodestones to construct their fortune-telling boards. The lodestones are made of an iron oxide and this aligns itself in a north–south direction. Now lodestones are being used for a new and popular path-finding invention called the "compass." This one has a spoon–shaped lodestone to indicate the direction.

LIGHT UP THE SKY!!!

Gunpowder was invented way back in the 9th century as a potion to help the emperor live forever. But today, there are very exciting developments for the man in the street. If you pack gunpowder into a long bamboo case and light a fuse, the whole thing will explode in fire and color! These "fireworks" are becoming the latest thing for any public show or entertainment. They can also be used for scaring away an enemy.

What's On in CHINATOWN?

★ ★ ★ ★ ☆

SINGING OUT!

Can you sing, play an instrument, act, and dance? Then why not join the Chinese opera and become a performer or "disciple of the pear garden" (the first Chinese opera troupe was called "Pear Garden"). You will be taught how to wear face makeup and do amazing stunts on stage. Different regions of China have different opera styles, so you will also have to decide where you want to live and perform.

Shadow sensation!

People are flocking to a new show in town—shadow puppets. It is said that they were invented to console Wu, emperor of the Han, when a favorite friend died. One of his ministers saw children playing with dolls and their shadows, and a popular new entertainment was born!

★ ☆ ★ ☆ ★

There's never a dull moment on the Chinese cultural scene. Here is a guide to what is happening in Chinese entertainment.

Tuning in

We Chinese love our music! It is played in the imperial court and at banquets and special ceremonies. The Imperial Music Bureau was established in the Qin Dynasty (221–7 BCE) to supervise court and military music. It also decides what folk music is acceptable. Instruments, such as bells and this hand drum (right), are very popular.

Moving it

Knowing how important health is to our readers, *HAIL!* has investigated the martial arts. They can be divided into external and internal disciplines. Kung Fu is an external fighting style that uses physical strength and speed to overcome an opponent. Tai Chi is an internal martial art that uses balance and sensitivity. It exploits the opponent's force against them.

Did you know?
Xiangsheng is a type of comedy performed as a monologue.

ON THE STAGE?

Since the Yuan Dynasty (1271–1368), Chinese opera has been encouraged by court officials and emperors. Indeed, the opera has become very fashionable and is performed in tea rooms, restaurants, and even in the open air. There are many different Chinese entertainments apart from opera, and they are all worth a visit. For example, the local troupe of jugglers and acrobats have just been invited to perform for members of the imperial court!

UNDER NEW
MANAGEMENT
THE MONGOLS

Over a period of six decades, the Mongols invaded and conquered ancient China. As early as 1206 CE, the fierce leader Genghis Khan had united the Mongol peoples across Central Asia and swept into China.

HERE COME THE MONGOLS

Genghis Khan did not let the Great Wall of China stop his rampage. His armed soldiers were famous as fierce fighters, particularly on horseback (left). Genghis Khan captured the northern parts of China and established his rule there. By 1260, his grandson, Kublai Khan, had become Emperor of China. By 1279, Kublai Khan had founded the powerful Yuan Dynasty (1271–1368) and taken over southern China.

"
If my body dies, let my body die, but do not let my country die.
"

Who is Genghis?

Genghis Khan's real name is Temujen. He was born in either 1162 or 1167, the son of a powerful Mongol chieftain. When he united the Mongol peoples in 1206, he took the title of Genghis Khan, which means "emperor of all emperors."

EXCLUSIVE!

HAIL! caught up with 12-year-old Kiyat, who has been working as Kublai Khan's stable boy for the last year. Here is what he had to say about the great leader.

So, what is life like working in the stables of the great Khan?

I can't complain. As you know, we Mongols love our horses, and it is up to me to keep the Khan's many steeds in great shape. But living in a palace—you can't beat that!

What's your boss like as a person?

Well, he does have a reputation as a tough guy. And it's true! I mean, how do you overrun most of Asia and still remain a nice guy?

We've heard he has had a special visitor lately, right?

Right—the Italian guy, Marco Polo. I think he was really impressed by what he saw here. I don't think many Europeans know much about China. But that will change now that Marco has gone back to Italy to tell people about what he found here!

Down with exams!

The Mongols are not big fans of the Confucian system of education or Chinese scholars in general. They have gotten rid of the exam system that we have used for many years to pick government officials. What next!?

Did you know?

Dadu, Kublai Khan's capital, was chosen in the Ming Dynasty (1368–1644) to be the site of the imperial palace, or Forbidden City (below left).

KUBLAI KHAN'S LEGACY

Kublai Khan encouraged Chinese scholarship and arts. Although he favored Tibetan Buddhism, he tolerated other religions. He received foreign visitors such as Marco Polo in his magnificent palace in the capital city of Dadu (now Beijing, left).

FINES 5¢ PER DAY FOR OVERDUE BOOKS

alchemist A scientist in medieval times who tried to turn base metals into gold

ancestor A person from whom one is descended, a forefather

archaeologist A scientist who examines the physical remains of past human life and culture

banish To force someone to leave their country

barracks Buildings used to lodge soldiers

charismatic Having special charm or appeal that inspires loyalty or enthusiasm in others

civilization The culture and society of a specific time and place

compass An instrument used to determine directions using a magnetized needle

deities Gods or goddesses

erosion The wearing away of Earth's surface by the action of water, glaciers, winds, waves, etc

exploits Striking or notable deeds or feats

imperial Relating to the rule of an empire by an emperor or group

irrigation The supply of water to crops by the use of pipes, ditches, canals, or streams

magnetized Caused an object to become magnetic

martial art Combat or self-defense activity such as karate or tae kwon do

mausoleum A tomb or burial place

nomad A person with no permanent home who moves with the seasons to find food and shelter

oracle A person who is said to be able to predict the future

paddy field An irrigated or flooded field where rice is grown

pagoda A temple or sacred building that usually has a tower with several different stories

philosophy A system of thoughts and beliefs, shared by a group of people

regimes Describes a ruler or family of rulers in command of a nation or group of people

silt Earth and fine sand that is carried by moving water and deposited as sediment

veneration Honor, respect, or worship, usually of a relative or god

yin and yang The opposing and balanced forces in Chinese philosophy

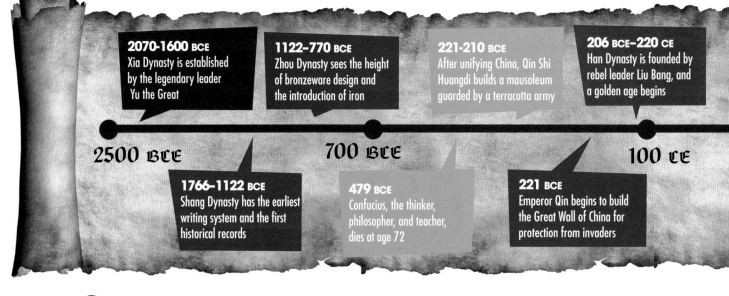

2070-1600 BCE
Xia Dynasty is established by the legendary leader Yu the Great

1122-770 BCE
Zhou Dynasty sees the height of bronzeware design and the introduction of iron

221-210 BCE
After unifying China, Qin Shi Huangdi builds a mausoleum guarded by a terracotta army

206 BCE–220 CE
Han Dynasty is founded by rebel leader Liu Bang, and a golden age begins

2500 BCE

700 BCE

100 CE

1766-1122 BCE
Shang Dynasty has the earliest writing system and the first historical records

479 BCE
Confucius, the thinker, philosopher, and teacher, dies at age 72

221 BCE
Emperor Qin begins to build the Great Wall of China for protection from invaders

ON THE INTERNET

Everything you need to know about ancient Chinese inventions and accomplishments
www.educ.uvic.ca/faculty/mroth/438/CHINA/CHINA-PAGE.html

Ancient Chinese recipes for kids to try for themselves
www.buzzle.com/articles/ancient-chinese-food-recipes-for-kids.html

All aspects of life in ancient China
www.historyforkids.org/learn/china/

Ancient China through the ages with timelines and maps
www.mnsu.edu/emuseum/prehistory/china/

Social studies site that looks at all aspects of life in ancient China
www.socialstudiesforkids.com/subjects/ancientchina.htm

Science, math, and astronomy in ancient China
www.historyforkids.org/learn/china/science/index.htm

Daily life in ancient China
http://china.mrdonn.org/

Explore this Internet search guide that helps you do research on ancient China
http://cybersleuth-kids.com/sleuth/History/Ancient_Civilizations/China/

BOOKS

China: True Books by Mel Friedman (Children's Press (CT), 2008)

Life in Ancient China by Paul Challen (Crabtree, 2004)

China: Land of Dragons and Emperors by Adeline Yen Mah (Delacorte Books for Young Readers, 2009)

The Big Book of China: A Guided Tour Through 5,000 Years of History by Qicheng Wang (Long River Press, 2010)

If I Were a Kid in Ancient China by Cobblestone Publishing (Cricket Books, 2007)

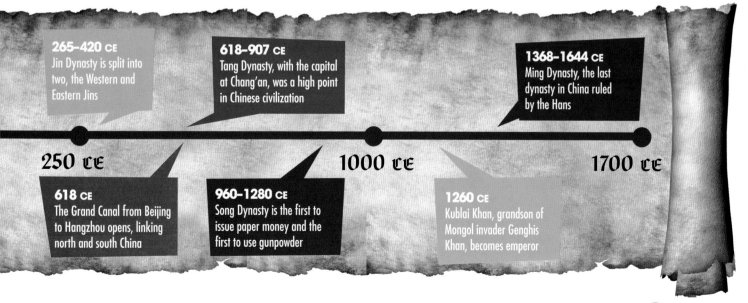

265–420 CE
Jin Dynasty is split into two, the Western and Eastern Jins

618–907 CE
Tang Dynasty, with the capital at Chang'an, was a high point in Chinese civilization

1368–1644 CE
Ming Dynasty, the last dynasty in China ruled by the Hans

250 CE

1000 CE

1700 CE

618 CE
The Grand Canal from Beijing to Hangzhou opens, linking north and south China

960–1280 CE
Song Dynasty is the first to issue paper money and the first to use gunpowder

1260 CE
Kublai Khan, grandson of Mongol invader Genghis Khan, becomes emperor

INDEX